Love, Life and Tragedy

Ink From A Bleeding Heart

Written by

Jon Burgess

A book of poetry written of life's heartbreaks and empowerments through the eyes of a man.

You can meet the Author at:
http://www.facebook.com/jon.burgess.9

Cover Design, Artwork, Interior Graphics and Formatting by True Beginnings Publishing. To contact the publisher, please write to the address:

true_beginnings_publishing@yahoo.com

Ordering Information:
To order additional copies of this book, please visit Amazon, or:
https://www.createspace.com/4528954

ISBN-13: 978-0615923826
ISBN-10: 0615923828

PRINTED IN THE UNITED STATES OF AMERICA

Table of Contents

~ DEDICATION ~

TO ALL THOSE WHO HAVE, ARE, OR
EVER WILL PLAY A ROLE IN MY LIFE....

IT MATTERS NOT HOW BIG OR SMALL
THE ROLE PLAYED.... ONLY THAT IN
SOME WAY, YOU HAVE MOLDED WHO I
WAS, AM, AND WILL BE.

Love

Seeing all in each other,

Yet seeing nothing,

Each and every flaw,

seen as a perfection.

It seems the more we know,

the less we are aware.

As if the others flaws

somehow make them perfect.

The Talk

I had a conversation today,

as I plod along my happy way.

Traipsing along with the work day done,

Relishing time in the glorious sun!

It had been a good spell since my last walk,

So I decided myself and I should talk.

And so we began to conversate,

about the greatest of things did contemplate.

We began to speak of love and hate,

and thus began a great debate.

What is it that causes such a feeling,

and what makes either one appealing?

How it is mankind dare treat one another,

That some would kill their own brother or mother.

Or how a man could love a woman so much,

He perceives he would die without feeling her touch?

The discussion continued as we did walk,

the answers to many a question we sought.

But seek the solution hard as we might,

It soon became clear it was a futile fight.

Then finally we realized we were both inept,

and some things you must simply accept.

For no matter time nor distance plod,

Some things are known only to God.

And suddenly we were filled with such peace;

Life once again had a new lease.

To know the solution there was no hurry,

For the answer is simply not to worry.

Teenagers

Why a struggle such it be,

those awkward teenage years?

I think I must forget my tea,

and slam a couple beers.

The drama seems to never end,

there seems no middle ground.

Their hearts are either on the mend,

or puppy love does pound.

They always want this or that,

and if they are denied...

They claim unloved or we think them fat,

I swear my brain is fried!

I know my consoling thought is errant,

of this I can't deny.

Just wait one day when you're a parent,

Is all I can reply.

Runaway

You look with terror in your eyes,
at what may someday be.
Your heart's been filled with hurts and lies,
you simply want to flee.

The past has not been kind to you,
each man was just a louse.
Now to yourself you must stay true,
new flames you quickly douse.

There really is no truth you say,
in what a man might speak.
It is a game you will not play,
so tears you will not leak.

I beg to differ just a bit,
and wish to prove you wrong.
There is a man with ample wit,
Who's loved you all along.

He is not perfect this he knows,

he simply cannot be.

Despite it though he learns and grows,

and prays that you will see.

To him, you are a perfect rose,

he cannot find one flaw.

Each day his love can only grow,

it is his sacred law.

His love for you is so intense

a never-ending fire.

He'd give his life recompense,

if hurt he did conspire.

So look into his eyes so deep,

forever he will stay.

Then drift off into peaceful sleep.

but do not run away.

To Love or Be Loved

I pondered to myself one day,

of the greater human need...

Which was more important

to the existence of the soul?

Is it to be loved?...

To feel love unconditionally,

a feeling beyond any other...

A sense of passion that eternal beget only of
another…

Or is it to love?...

To give of yourself completely and fully...

No thoughts of restraint,

nor of ramification...

Knowing full well it may be unrequited and
vexatious...

Yet caring not.

Oh, such anguish this conundrum doth bring...

what a travail of the mind...

or is it of the heart, or the soul?

How does one choose which is of more
consequence...

or upon which to focus?

And yet in absolute truth, no conundrum exists...

For if one has the courage

to look deep within...

and the patience to peel away the layers...

Only then do you find

than in all reality

there is no separation...

You cannot know one

without knowing the other...

So dependent and intertwined

are they upon one another neither can exist alone.

And yet we try, oh do we try...

And thus begat hate....

Strife

Sitting this still morn in the silence,

not a sound to be heard in this place.

In my head a battle of violence,

As the thoughts in my head pound and race!

Why, how, what does it all mean,

in this whirlwind we call life.

Just one thing to me it seems,

Life's sole meaning is but strife.

So, strife, bring your best thing,

bring it on-the best of your pain.

But in the end you make no gain,

For I will learn to dance in the rain.

The Dream

Sleep doth elude me... my thoughts perpetual

as in the stillness, I lie.

Thoughts of you,

overwhelming my mind...

consuming my totality.

Eyes fade and lids close

as if I can deny them...

but their pursuit is relentless.

Images play before me...

painting beautiful tapestries

on the canvas of my mind.

A warm sunny afternoon

when first we met...

A cold drink and a warm heart,

a perfect "Rockwell" day.

The evening I held you in my arms,

and in your pain gave reassurance

until your anguish soothed...

Oh, how my heart was twinge.

Or the morning we first made love...

Our bodies enmeshed as one,

Indistinguishable each from the other,

our pleasures intermingled.

I reach out to hold you,

but you are long since gone.

Were you ever really there?

or is this all just a dream?

A blissful...sleepless...dream....

Senses

Be still my savage heart...

You beat wildly within me at the thought of her.

Visions of her haunt me,

as a vapor in the night...

I feel as though she is with me,

her very presence tangible...

denying every known law

of space and time.

I feel her warm breath

upon the nape of my neck...

Quickly I turn to see her but she is not there.

Sweet whispers pull me...

drawn to a destination,

but I find only the masses.

I sit wearily and close my eyes...

Taste her sweet lips upon mine,

but it is only heaven's mist.

The smell of her sweet perfume

reveals only potted jasmines

in the marketplace.

What spell has been cast...

that I should discern her,

every sense constantly tantalized

with no regard of her absence.

I feel as though losing my senses,

yet they have never been more alive...

And suddenly I realize...

I am not losing my mind...

I am losing my heart...

For this is love.

Perfection Demise

Perfect in every way,

not one flaw...

Gorgeous beyond compare

and more valuable than

any gem....

So gentle of spirit,

Finally vulnerable once again,

yet he squashed her....

Like a beautiful butterfly

on a windshield...

And seeing this...

He was never the same, again.

Ponderings on Heaven

I know in Heaven someday I'll be,

of this I surely know.

At last my spirit will be set free,

and on my way I'll go.

Although my time on Earth isn't done,

I cannot help but think.

What do you do in Heaven for fun?

besides praise, eat, and drink.

Are there billiards and darts and football?

or any other sport?

Do the folks from the south still say y'all,

during a grand retort?

We know that there will be no more war,

the world shall see a tryst.

So will anyone be too upset,

to lose a game of Risk?

And what about all the feasts, oh drat,

and never getting full.

Eating it all without getting fat,

it never could get dull.

So many questions surge through my mind,

they tumble to and fro.

Pondering on the wonders I'll find,

but just one thing I know...

Gone forever are illness and pain,

so too the beggar's hand.

Forever our Mighty God will reign,

and with Him we will stand.

The Flame

What once began one moonlit eve,

so many blessed years ago.

Neither one could ever conceive,

what from a friendship soon would grow.

It seemed the years did quickly pass,

with each one closer they became.

But with the end of school alas,

their paths were simply not the same.

And so they went their separate ways,

each one to follow what they dreamed.

'Tween visits they would count the days,

Far too many it often seemed.

Several years did come and go,

their longing became much stronger.

And finally they both did know,

they could be apart no longer.

It's been fifty years since the day,

when to each other said their vow.

They don't forget one single day,

to speak of their love even now.

And so you see the best of friends,

were never meant to stay the same.

From friendship love that never ends!

They became an eternal flame.

Storms

Storms raging....

Winds ripping and shredding

as the rain pounds, relentless...

cold, icy, and unforgiving,

Cover he seeks....

The search frantic but futile,

Tissue and bone begin to ache...

and strength quickly fades.

Yet shining is the sun......

Superman

I am but a simple man,

Comprised of flesh and bone!

Trying to do the best I can,

as I face this world alone.

My journey is not a simple one,

and quite often it's a trial.

Many battles have I done,

and I'll be fighting for a while.

I'll fight ferocious every day,

for what I believe is right.

No one shall divert my way,

be it sunshine or dark of night.

So on I fight day after day,

with trials and disease.

Try to show just one the way,

for that I'll hit my knees.

I fight a different evil you see,

but I will fight with all I can.

For superhuman I may never be,

but always a superman.

Second Chance

Disheveled and perturbed,

the darkened alley I wandered...

humbled and broken of spirit.

Ruminating on deeds of old,

like an old black and white movie

playing in my mind's eye...

What cruel twist of fate

had brought me to this place

of such dark contemplation?

Scenes played out one by one,

the tears flow as a river...

cascading down my cheeks.

Each tribulation tears at me,

as though my heart be flagellated...

each stripe deeper than before.

My anguish far from complete,

the scenes turn away from me...

to those I cannot bear to watch.

Scenes of such egregious offenses,

perpetrated by none other than myself.

Such travail have I caused,

often to those most beloved...

I cogitate over their wounds,

and the flagellation persists...

chunks now torn from my heart

as I see their agony.

Forgiveness I beg of them,

from some it comes not...

from some in abundance,

and I am humbled at their feet.

In that moment...

In that gracious act of love...

Comes the realization that

it is never too late for a second chance...

Senseless

Do you not know the pain you caused?

Awakened from peaceful slumber,

to have my world shattered and paused

by such a senseless act...

What were you thinking of that night?

Surely of no one but yourself...

Precious memories now hidden from sight,

Overshadowed now only by tragedy...

Your senseless act of selfishness...

Left me as collateral damage!

To suffer the eternal questions

For which I have no answers…

You were sick we all knew...

But hope we never lost.

Until that eerie silent night,

you gave up no matter the cost.

Twenty six years it has been

since that fateful night.

Yet now I have to face it too,

and I can't describe the fright.

The wound has been reopened,

at times my life seems paused...

Grandpa you really have no idea,

how much pain you caused....

The Promised Land

I wander about in the darkness,

that which appears to be my life...

There is nothing sure here,

not even my very next step...

Will I land sure footed,

or fall off some precipice...

Launching into some depthless abyss,

never again to be heard or spoken of...

As if in fact I had never existed,

on this plane or any other...

There is no luminance here,

as I strain to see my future...

Which cavernous path to choose,

to lead me to my desired haven...

I push forward into the darkness,

knowing there is no other way...

Going onward is my only hope,

that in time I will arrive in its peace...

Rare it seems is the correct choice,

often finding only more darkness...

The occasional glimpse of light,

this is all that sustains my spirit...

I cry out to God to lead me,

to carry me to some peaceful place...

My cries echo in the stillness,

and I wonder if He hears me...

And yet if I simply rest and listen,

I can hear the occasional whisper...

His sacred voice urging me on,

assuring me of His faithfulness...

Pushing forward and trusting now,

for I know it is in His time...

Then I shall break through the dark,

and into that place of rest...

And in that moment a thought,

to look back upon my journey...

In doing so a revelation of sorts,

which had eluded me to this point...

Looking back, I can clearly see,

all that had been in the purest light...

In my journey there were no missteps,

for all had to be taken to arrive here...

The Promised Land.

Above **O**dds

Hearts so close,

yet distance so far.

Such yearning neither

time nor space comprehend.

Above all odds,

things never imagined.

Two souls as one,

intertwined beyond separation.

Scars

I thought upon a wound I had,

and how it had to drain.

For just a moment made me sad,

as I focused on the pain.

We thought that I was healing well,

had made it through the worst.

When suddenly it went to hell,

I could swear that I was cursed.

The scar itself quite nice in size,

finally healed I was hoping.

So just imagine my surprise,

when it suddenly burst open.

Eruption brought forth exudate,

first bloody then just clear.

At first there was no pain to rate,

only a modicum of fear.

But as I sat today in thought,

whilst pondering this strife.

It all became quite clear to me,

that such the same is life.

With hurt in life we've had to deal,

with scars left from the pain.

And just as wounds begin to heal,

they burst open once again.

But take comfort in those painful scars,

that you can never heal.

The One who can is above the stars,

and you simply have to kneel.

The Trip

I long to take a trip one day,

to visit a land so far away.

A place that yet remains unseen,

where everything is pure and clean.

A land where every day is bright,

even in the dark of night.

Where not one creature isn't free!

roaming amongst both you and me.

A world where we put people first,

and not one child has hunger or thirst.

There is no need for a beggar's hand,

as united we are to work the land.

A place where poignant color flows,

as all of nature's beauty shows.

Pollution is of no concern,

for the lesson we did finally learn.

A land in which there is no need,

for politicians or their greed.

Where common folk no longer cower,

no more need have we for power.

A world where time just has no use,

the very concept is quite obtuse.

When at least it seems we finally know,

life's true joy is in the ebb and flow.

It is really quite the trip you see,

this wonderland where I wish to be.

So far away but so easy to find,

kept safe away in the back of my mind.

The Beast

The mighty beast stalks...

with eerie stealth he pursues,

undetected in the shadows.

Evil plans he will soon ordain...

for he has but one desire...

to drain life from his victims,

and end their will to survive.

In silence he conspires...

a perfectionist at destruction,

he devises the perfect scheme.

With the utmost patience he waits...

and at the perfect moment besets,

his gaze paralyzing in terror.

His victim once majestic,

now lies helpless before him...

life-force draining as blood.

Ravenous jaws clench on flesh,

and consciousness fades.

Life, love, and dreams vanish...

taken by a beast of unlimited power,

And yet with no power at all...

lest to him it be given.

The beast, you see, is known to us all,

For he dwells within each of us!

He is us... using us... against us...

His name...

The Past.

Prayer

I fall in desperation to my knees,

crying out to Him in my darkness...

Oh Father God I pray,

tears cascading down my cheeks...

Only you know me, Oh Lord,

my innermost being.

From you there is no hiding..

you know every thought

and every wickedness inside me.

You know every failure,

and every pain I have caused.

I am not worthy to be called yours...

In my brokenness I hear your voice,

whispering deep within my soul.

Oh, my precious child...

You were known to me

since the beginning of time.

I knew all that you would become,

and in you find no flaw...

your ransom long paid.

I know the desires of your heart,

pure desires in an impure world...

Your pain grieves me so,

but trust in Me you must...

A glorious plan I have for you,

paradise once through storm...

And finding solace...

I sleep.

Writer's Block

Thoughts and words run 'round my brain,

I can't get them out no matter the pain.

Even the ones that make me feel happy,

stay locked inside no matter how sappy.

Page after page I scribble and scribble,

but pen nothing more than moronic dribble.

If sense in these thoughts soon I don't find,

I am truly in fear of losing my mind.

Oh Dear Lord I cry, beg, and plead,

to put them to paper is all that I need.

Send me an Angel to guide as I write,

so my dreams will not be tortured tonight.

And so it was that this poem came,

as much as it may sound really lame.

I thought to myself, "Oh what the F*ck,

you can always scribe on Writer's Block."

Wake Me

Wake me up I plead!

Rouse me from my slumber...

cease the torment of my mind.

Pain and suffering endless abounds...

men, women, and children,

all feeling the same despondence.

Trudging wearily day after day,

feeling void and empty...

as though they will never be good enough.

Degradation pounded into brains,

told they are subpar from youth...

efforts soon become meaningless.

Children scoffed at for a test graded "C",

taught early that average is pathetic...

and that a 70 is unworthy of praise.

College youth must close their minds...

they must conform to the status quo,

for the days of free thinking are dead.

Then, once grown up a slave become...

they must be silent and submit to their work,

for freedom and dreams are a myth.

Pushed far beyond all endurance,

their spirits shattered and broken...

they fall silently into enslavement.

How long a suffering before we see

that our ways are erroneous...

the oppressions we place on ourselves and others?

When shall we cast aside our shackles...

burst forth with free minds and absolute love?

Somebody wake me up, I plead!

And then, in great sadness I realize...

I have been awake all along...

The Fall

My gaze falls upon thee...

the splendor of a goddess,

and grace of an angel...

Breath deserts me,

my strength abandoned...

That you take human form

befuddles me...

for your glory such form

cannot contain.

I am swept away...

your words hypnotize, and your spell is cast.

My fall has begun...

it was inevitable from first glance.

No question left in my mind,

save one consequential...

Will you reach out

and take me by the hand...

with your gentle strength

pull me safely into you...

Or will your hand withdraw,

as I fall upon the rocks below...

mocking as my lifeblood drains?

Choose as you will my enchantress...

For simply having envisioned thee,

Victory is mine.

Sin

Disgrace, abhorrent, abomination

are words so easily said.

As if to spout such degradation,

might change things in their head.

We look upon our fellow man,

our faces full of disdain.

And judge him 'cause we think we can,

with not one clue to his pain.

It matters not what he's been through,

we do not really care.

He is the one who chose to do,

the things he shouldn't dare.

Murder, rape, cheat or lie...

which of them is worse?

For which one ought a man to die,

or suffer eternal curse?

The answer is rather simple see,

and really not that odd.

It really should be you and me,

In the Holy eyes of God.

But for just one thing we be spared,

if you take a moment to think.

Jesus gave His life and dared,

to bring us from the brink.

But if we continue to spew such thought,

not one of us shall win.

For passing judgment for sins long bought,

is in itself a sin!

Stronger

I stood out in the sun today,

and thought upon my life.

Pondered on the price I pay,

and the value of the strife.

My mind to as a child went,

the suffering that was mental.

To put me down my dad was bent,

yet it only made me gentle.

A few years in the Army when,

but by illness almost died.

Death could not take me then,

though three times he did try.

No more a soldier home I went,

feeling burdened with a curse.

The next 4 years in school I spent,

and hence became a nurse.

Then I married... raised my kid,

at times the fights were loud.

Failed though the marriage did,

of my daughter I am proud.

Still a young man I did consider,

when at first I got the news.

The cancer could have made me bitter,

but helped change so many views.

Now looking back upon the price,

A debate there is no longer.

For I would gladly pay it thrice,

it has only made me stronger.

Obamacare

There once was a man named Obama,

whose Presidency caused quite a drama.

Reform in the Supreme Court passed,

and many a folk were madly aghast.

So many voices so angry and loud,

you could hear them above any old crowd.

Not from just one side or the other,

but both sides pitting brother on brother.

The insults did fly and the insanity grew,

I just prayed it wouldn't infect me or you.

Some were so happy they only could cry,

others so indignant they wanted to die.

They argued the legislation was bad,

that in it was nothing good to be had.

Coverage for a condition was wrong,

pre-existing it didn't matter how long.

You know this will only drive up the cost,

and healthcare as we know is lost.

Insurance moguls will now rule the day,

and take even larger chunks of our pay.

The argument I think has one big flaw,

so much focus being placed on the law.

Instead of us making a cry or a sob,

let us scrutinize the Insurance Mob.

They've gotten away with so much for so long,

by feeding us all a dance and a song.

It's about time that we take them to task,

and quit sipping Cool Aid out of our flask.

So let's quit trying to start us a war,

look deeper and see what the true fight is for.

Now as Forrest would say in a brief tit for tat

That's all that I have to say about that.

The One

Long ago and far away,

and before time had begun.

Father God had set the day,

I'd finally find the one.

A woman with a heart of gold,

and the purest of spirits too.

In the pursuit of justice bold,

fighting fearlessly for the few.

Putting others above herself,

never giving a second thought.

While her needs sat upon a shelf,

love by her sacrifice she taught.

The beauty of an angel's glow,

Radiates from the inside out.

She is the one I seem to know,

for in my mind there is no doubt.

You ask me who this woman be,

or if she ever ever knew?

Silly woman you do not see,

that I am speaking about you!

Never Forget

It seems to me like yesterday,

and yet it's been awhile.

Now eleven years to the day,

an act of terror so vile.

We woke together on that morn,

to go about our day.

Then suddenly our hearts were torn,

and sunny skies were gray.

We watched the Towers as they fell,

crumpled to Ground Zero.

Amongst the ashes and the smell,

many were a hero.

The Pentagon was then hit next,

terror clearly at our door.

And we became a nation vexed,

and swore there'd be no more.

That brings us to flight 93,

that Pennsylvania field.

They sacrificed for you and me,

and told us never yield.

And so I sit, reflect, and write,

on one thing you can bet.

For Freedom we must always fight;

and in our stance be set.

Dedicated to all those lost on 9/11/01 and their loved ones.

NEVER FORGET

Prison

Why is it I cannot be free,

I'm trapped within these chains.

Forever bound I'm meant to be,

amidst these joys and pains.

At times I struggle and I fight,

most oft to no avail.

For all my strength and all my might,

I cannot help but fail.

This prison is like none you see,

Its walls you cannot break.

Impervious they seem to be,

although they are but fake.

You see it is my love for you,

which keeps me ever bound.

And though it be a prison true,

No better one be found.

Soulmate

Two strangers meet by random chance,

although from worlds apart.

No thought to give a second glance,

or risk a wounded heart.

To many pains both have endured,

from lovers in the past.

They swear no way they can be cured,

the thought sets them aghast.

And so they go their separate ways,

it seems this is the end.

They wonder just how many days,

their hearts will need to mend.

Back they go to their daily grind,

there seems no end in sight.

Yet always on each other's mind,

for "something" felt so right.

So one day they begin to talk,

despite their horrid fears.

Then side by side begin to walk,

and wipe away their tears.

The years go by and feelings grow,

no longer is their doubt.

It seems indeed they finally know,

what true love is about.

So when you think you cannot love,

It is not chance but fate.

For God will send you from above,

your one and true soul mate.

The Spirit

Into the emptiness my spirit bellows...

unheard even in the stillness of night.

Wandering through the eerie darkness,

the blackness which is my own soul...

Seeking the light so desperately desired,

though overwhelmed by the shadows.

For so long my spirit has sought the light,

longing to be pure in love once more...

To bury the skeletons of the past,

And vanquish the slayers of the heart...

Pile their corpses one on another,

and climb over these impervious walls.

My spirit's life-force grows weary now,

the will to fight now drained...

The heavy burden becomes too much,

not even a hero could bear its toll...

Slowly, eyes close and vision dims,

a final glimpse,

and I spot you in the shadows...

And my spirit is renewed.

Catalyst

My heart yearns incessantly

for the catalyst once mine...

For shackled I was,

enslaved in errant thought.

Falsehoods held as true...

a sane insanity

that was once my life.

So many changes she begat...

overwhelming, at first.

The contortions of my mind...

painful and excruciating,

yet the freedom of thought

spawning such pleasure...

Craving more day by day.

An addiction it became...

Its dominion no longer an option,

but a necessity.

Its vigor consumes me,

my shackles fractured.

Free now is my mind,

sanity and clarity of thought

never before known...

I long for my catalyst now lost,

but her power still remains...

Everlasting.

Great Wall

You don't see the conflict within you,

the strife between heart and mind...

A contest raging endlessly,

so as to fracture you from within.

Your heart yearns to feel the flames,

to be swept away in blinding fury...

longing to find a kindred soul

whose passion not only parallels,

but exceeds your own.

Yet you are bound...

Bound by ancient tribulations,

beget of those you once loved...

Those in whom trust once placed,

and then made desolate.

And so it began...

Day by day...

Brick by brick...

Oh, how you recalled each hurt,

as to each its own venue you placed.

Each day, week, month, year...

You toiled away with sweat and blood

as you raised up each layer...

So determined was your subconscious

to shield you from torment,

it forbid you to even ascertain

so that you could not interfere.

So strong now is the encumbrance,

Even the Great Wall is no rival...

How can I ensure the demise

of so stout a defense

that you do not even fathom?

Like the Great Wall...

Brick by brick, many years it

would take...

But for you I would take a lifetime.

Brain Freeze

Thoughts race endlessly,

tearing through the tendrils of the mind.

Seemingly out of control

as they weave in and out,

around and through...

Blazing through the brain,

through every fiber...

every synapse...

Seeming to be no end.

Control seems lost,

memories, hopes, dreams...

Flooding...

Overwhelming...

Crashing through the mind,

Each demanding its own special place...

Each trying to cast the other aside,

so as to be all consuming...

until past, present, and future blend...

Indistinguishable from one another...

And the brain freezes....

Diamond

I lived my life upon this Earth,

a struggle day to day.

And often questioned my own worth,

or the game that I did play.

A fight it's been for my whole life,

from youth up until now.

Constant living in horrid strife,

and all I could think is "Wow".

My childhood to "dad" a game,

he couldn't let me be.

Every problem to me the blame,

I am a child was my plea.

Told I was never good enough,

and that I was a louse.

Made me on the outside tough,

but timid as a mouse.

All my life its impact had,

on everything I had done.

To many of them had turned out bad,

and seldom had I won.

Then, one day, it came to me,

he no longer had such power.

And from the darkness I did see,

the Light that very hour.

I knew that moment in the end,

I was the captain of my soul.

And on the help of many a friend,

became a diamond out of coal.

Life

Why must we live our life a rush,

and do everything in a hurry?

Our souls the burdens of life do crush,

as to and fro we scurry.

Each and every morning, we wake,

and drag weary bodies from bed.

Our lifeblood from us the stress does take,

'till, one day, we wake up dead.

When the workday is finally done,

It's homeward we do trod.

Way too tired to think of fun,

we sit and our heads do nod.

Finally, the weekend is here,

the next two days are free.

But life in the fast lane makes it clear,

there is no time to just "be".